AF584429

Explorers of Australia

Volume 2

Explorers From 1788 to the Present

Linsie Tan

First published 2017 by
Redback Publishing
PO Box 357 Frenchs Forest NSW 2086
Australia

ISBN 978-1-9256301-9-0

Author: Linsie Tan
Editor: Jane Tara
Original illustrations © Redback Publishing 2017
Originated by Redback Publishing
Printed and bound in China by Leo Paper

Acknowledgements
Abbreviations: l—left, r—right, b—bottom, t—top, c—centre, m—middle
We would like to thank the following for permission to reproduce photographs:
coverpage t The Sturt Expedition out of food and water / Percy Leason, National Library of Australia, nla.obj-134285365, p4 http://sydneylivingmuseums.com.au. Summerdrought, p13 NASA and Jeremy Buckingham via Wikimedia Commons, p14 State Library of VIC, p18 National Library of Australia, PIC/9259 LOC Negatives cabinet PIC/9259, p19 Portrait of John Oxley, 1783-1828, nla.obj-137044418, p19 - By Summerdrought (Own work) [CC BY-SA 4.0 (http://creativecommons.org/licenses/by-sa/4.0)], via Wikimedia Commons, p20 Mitchell Library, State Library of New South Wales, p29 - By NASA [Public domain], via Wikimedia Commons.

Every effort has been made to contact copyright holders of any material reproduced in this book. Any omissions will be rectified in subsequent printings if notice is given to the publisher.

National Library of Australia Cataloguing-in-Publication entry

Creator: Tan, Linsie, author.
Title: Explorers from 1788 to the Present / Linsie Tan.
ISBN: 9781925630190 (hardback)
Series: Tan, Linsie. Explorers of Australia ; vol. 2
Target Audience: For primary school age
Subjects: Explorers--Australia--History--Juvenile literature.
Australia--Discovery and exploration.
Australia--History--Juvenile literature.

Contents

Exploring the First Settlement at Sydney

FRESH WATER AND FARMS

When the first settlement was founded at Sydney Cove in 1788, none of the new settlers knew anything about what lay beyond. They did not even know if Australia was an island, or if it was connected to New Guinea or Tasmania.

Governor Phillip immediately started to explore. His aims were to find fresh water and land suitable for planting crops. He was responsible for the safety of the settlement, so he also needed to ensure they were not under threat of attack from either the Aboriginal inhabitants or people from any foreign nation that may have landed in the colony without his knowledge. The British and French were on the verge of being at war with each other, and French explorer, La Perouse, had made a surprising appearance at Botany Bay at the same time that the British fleet arrived.

Three months after landing, Governor Phillip and his men rowed boats up the Parramatta River and found land which was later used for the site of a permanent Government House and for the first successful crop of wheat grown in the colony.

Right: A view of Sydney Cove. 1793
Above: Governor Phillip

CONVICTS AND CATTLE

While most exploration was official and ordered by the Governor, there were two unusual groups who set out on their own to explore. There were no jails at first, and convicts lived in tents. The only thing stopping them from running away into the bush was the fear of not knowing what lay beyond. A few adventurous convicts did escape, but most either died or gave up and returned to Sydney Cove. A few stole boats and got away.

Then there were the cattle that travelled on the ships to Sydney Cove along with the convicts. They escaped into the bush and were discovered years later by a convict who was well rewarded for finding them. The cattle had strayed a long way from the coast to an area west of Sydney which is still called the Cowpastures.

Above: Cattle in a paddock, 1930

Why did Britain have so many convicts?

- The Industrial Revolution was replacing thousands of farm workers with machinery. They travelled to London and other large cities looking for work, and many ended up living in desperate conditions.
- Improvements in agriculture had made the production of food more efficient and this caused the population of Britain to grow.
- Changes to the land ownership system in England had resulted in many people being expelled from their farms and houses.
- The outcome of these social and industrial events was that the large cities in England became very overcrowded.
- Lack of food, overcrowding and poverty led to an increase in crime.
- The American colonies had previously been used as a convict dumping ground, but the settlers there waged war on the British and drove them out. This resulted in Britain not being able to send convicts there after the 1770's.
- The British prisons were inadequate and many convicts were housed in rotting ships anchored in the Thames River.

Above: View inside a Convict Ship

Is Australia an Island?

MATTHEW FLINDERS AND GEORGE BASS

ALL AROUND AUSTRALIA

From 1801 to 1803, in command of HMS Investigator, Flinders became the first person to circumnavigate the whole of Australia. The expedition was financed by the Royal Navy with the aim of finding new trading opportunities and ports where British ships would have a safe harbour. Flinders was also ordered to improve the charts and therefore navigation in the region. The British knew the French were sailing around Australia and mapping it. Fearful this would lead to France claiming parts of the continent, the British were keen to know where the boundaries of the land actually were and whether there were places suitable for founding more settlements.

Left: Old world map
Above: Matthew Flinders

Above: Statue of Matthew Flinders and his cat

NAMING AUSTRALIA

The discovery that Australia is an island showed that it was not the fabled southern continent that scholars once believed existed. Flinders was the first person to use the name Australia for the island, including Tasmania in this term.

THE COAST NEAR SYDNEY

Matthew Flinders was a naval officer and George Bass was a ship's surgeon. In the 1790s, they both explored the coast from Sydney using a boat called Tom Thumb.

VAN DIEMEN'S LAND

People knew that Van Diemen's Land existed, but they did not know if it was connected to the mainland or not. Bass and Flinders sailed through Bass Strait in 1798, proving that Van Diemen's Land was not connected to the rest of Australia. The importance of this discovery was that ships could now use this route on their way from England, rather than taking the longer and more dangerous route around the southern tip of Tasmania.

EXPANDING SETTLEMENT

As a result of the discoveries made by Flinders and Bass, more settlements were established. The British initially only claimed the eastern part of Australia in 1770. In later years, they sent settlers to formally claim the western part as well, founding Albany in 1826 and the Swan River Settlement (later renamed Perth) in 1829.

TRIM THE CAT

Matthew Flinders' cat, Trim, sailed with him around the coast of Australia in 1801. Trim survived a shipwreck and was imprisoned with his owner by the French in Mauritius.

Exploring the Bush and the Rivers

The wide continent of Australia was a mystery to the European settlers. Although explorers had landed on the coast, none of them had ventured far inland. The inland exploration of Australia began in the early 1800s and continued for decades. Some of these journeys were organised as government funded expeditions. There were also private journeys that were paid for by the explorers themselves and their supporters.

Reasons for Inland Exploration

- Human curiosity
- The desire to own land
- The need to find more space for the growing population
- The need to grow food to feed the colony
- Rewards were sometimes offered by the government to explorers
- The search for mineral resources
- The need to find routes for roads, railways and telegraph communication lines

The Role of the Squatters

Below: The Squatter at Home, 1847

Thousands of hectares of the new lands found by the explorers were given to settlers. After 1831, this system changed, and new settlers had to pay the government for their land. So much land was being discovered that Governor Darling set limits to where settlers could go. Some settlers ignored this rule and 'squatted' on land beyond the boundaries set by the Governors, hoping they would eventually be given the right to claim it for themselves. These settlers became known as Squatters.

Assisting European Explorers

Aboriginal people frequently agreed to help the European explorers, acting as guides and translators. In many cases they showed the Europeans well-worn routes to make their journeys easier. For example, when Blaxland, Lawson and Wentworth crossed the Blue Mountains and discovered the plains beyond, they were probably shown the way by Aboriginal people. Ludwig Leichhardt also took two Aboriginal explorers with him on his last journey into the desert.

Although Edward Eyre is credited with being the first person to cross from South Australia to the Western Australian coast by land, he was accompanied all the way by an Aboriginal explorer named Wylie. Both men endured the same hardships and reached the Western Australian coast together.

Not all contact between Aboriginal people and European explorers was friendly. There are numerous records in explorers' journals of violent incidents occurring when Aboriginal people fought to expel the invaders from their lands.

Beyond the Blue Mountains in New South Wales

Until the colonists found a way to cross the Blue Mountains to the west of Sydney, they had no idea there were extensive plains suitable for pastures and crops, and large river systems for irrigation. The growing settlement needed more land, so Governor Macquarie encouraged explorers to find out what was over the mountains.

Above: Governor's House in the Township of Parramatta. 1798

BLAXLAND, LAWSON AND WENTWORTH

Gregory Blaxland, William Lawson and William Wentworth attempted to cross the Blue Mountains in 1813. They were landowners and therefore different from the naval officers who had been the explorers of the colony previously. Guided by Aboriginal people who agreed to show them the way, they reached Mount Blaxland, a hill near the present day town of Lithgow. They managed to cross the Blue Mountains by following the ridges of the hills, rather than descending into the valleys. Even today, bushwalkers frequently become lost in the interconnected network of valleys in the Blue Mountains.

Above: Crossing the Blue Mountains

GEORGE EVANS

In 1813, the surveyor, George Evans, went beyond the Blue Mountains and found the Macquarie River. Setting out again in 1815, he found the Lachlan River. These discoveries were important because they showed that there was enough water beyond the mountains to support agriculture. The route Evans took became the first road to the western farmlands. When the road was complete, settlement in the newly found areas soon expanded as land was granted to people who wanted to start farming there. In 1815, the town of Bathurst was founded to support the new settlers.

Above: George Evans, 1882

VIEW ON THE MACQUARIE RIVER,

Above: View on the Macquarie River, 1825

Above: Liverpool Plains today

JOHN OXLEY

In 1817, John Oxley, the Surveyor General of the colony of New South Wales, explored the new lands over the Blue Mountains, with the aim of finding out where the Lachlan River flowed. The next year he explored the course of the Macquarie River as well, and found the Liverpool Plains, the Castlereagh River, the Hastings River and Port Macquarie. The importance of these discoveries was that sources of water for farming were assured and settlers were encouraged to go there. Oxley believed the rivers flowed into an inland sea, a theory that was not disproved until many years later. The goal of discovering an inland sea in the centre of Australia attracted many explorers over the coming years.

Above: Portrait of John Oxley

Exploring Further Inland

Above: Allan Cunningham

ALLAN CUNNINGHAM

For many years, none of the settlers knew what lay to the north in the colony of New South Wales. In 1827, Allan Cunningham set out on an expedition to find out. He travelled north into what is now Queensland and discovered the Darling Downs, which became one of the most productive areas of farmland in the colony.

CHARLES THROSBY

From 1802 to 1821, Charles Throsby and his nephew, along with Joseph Wild and James Vaughan, explored inland New South Wales. They found the Limestone Plains, Lake George, the Molonglo River and the Murrumbidgee River. They reported that the plains would provide good pastures for sheep and cattle. Parts of the areas they found later became the site for Canberra and the Australian Capital Territory.

Below: Darling Downs today

THOMAS MITCHELL

Above: Thomas Mitchell, 1830

Thomas Mitchell was the colony's Surveyor-General after John Oxley died in 1828. From 1831 to 1836, he explored inland from Sydney and south to Victoria, charting the courses of a number of rivers, including the Murrumbidgee, Darling and Murray. In the south he discovered very promising farmland which he called Australia Felix. On reaching the Victorian coast, Mitchell was surprised to find that the Henty Brothers had already made a settlement there, having travelled by ship from Tasmania with all their livestock. The news of the excellent pastures Mitchell discovered soon encouraged drovers to take their herds to Victoria from New South Wales, driving them along the route that Mitchell had taken.

In 1845, Mitchell set out to find a route to the northern coast of Australia, at the same time that another explorer, Ludwig Leichhardt, was undertaking a similar journey. Mitchell did not reach anywhere near the northern coast, but he did find a number of rivers in central Queensland.

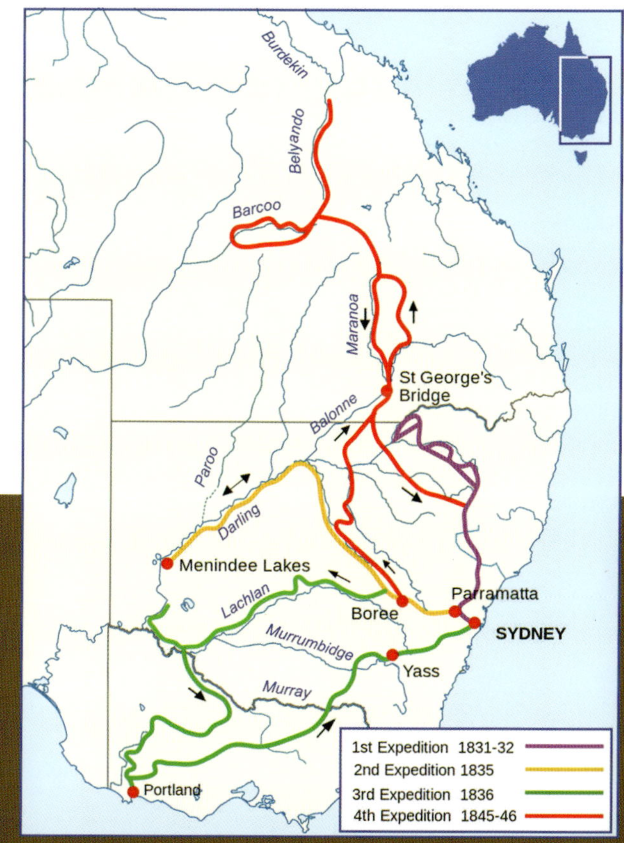

Right: The Expeditions of Thomas Mitchell

HAMILTON HUME AND WILLIAM HOVELL

Below: William Hovell, 1872

In 1824, Hume and Hovell explored south of Sydney, and on towards what was later the colony of Victoria. The two men sold their own valuables to raise the necessary funds for the expedition, although the government gave them some equipment for their journey. After crossing the Murrumbidgee River by pulling a raft across it with ropes, Hume and Hovell became the first Europeans to see the Australian Alps. Pushing on, they reached the southern coast at Port Phillip. Both men received large grants of land from the government when they returned. They had been responsible for finding large areas of grazing land and people soon started moving there, creating settlements and felling trees to provide grassland for their livestock.

PAUL EDMUND DE STRZELECKI

Above: Sir Paul Edmund de Strzelecki, 1874

Strzelecki was a Polish geologist who named the highest mountain in Australia, Mount Kosciuszko, in 1840. He was possibly the first man to discover gold in Australia, but the governor asked him to keep this quiet, to stop people leaving their farms and jobs to become gold prospectors. This would have ruined the small colony's economic development. Strzelecki compiled a geological survey of the colony of New South Wales, and published a book on his findings after returning to England. His book included the first large geological map of the colony, and his detailed observations covered geology, climate, fossils and wildlife. He also wrote a chapter describing the Aboriginal people.

WOMEN EXPLORERS

Most of the explorers of Australia were men. In the past, it was unusual for women to undertake dangerous journeys alone or lead teams of men.

Lady Jane Franklin

Jane Franklin climbed Mount Wellington and explored the rugged wilderness of Tasmania. In 1839, she travelled overland from Melbourne to Sydney, an extremely difficult and dangerous journey. She was the wife of the Lieutenant Governor of Tasmania.

Above: Emily Creaghe

Emily Creaghe

In 1882, Emily Creaghe explored the area along the Gulf of Carpentaria with her husband. They survived the tropical heat and lack of fresh water. Emily's endurance was made even more remarkable by the fact that she was pregnant at the time.

Above: Monument at the top of Mount Kosciuszko

Is there an inland sea?

CHARLES STURT

From 1828 to 1830, Charles Sturt explored NSW, intent on tracing the courses of the Macquarie River and the Murrumbidgee River. His team then followed the Murray River almost to the ocean near the site of Adelaide, but they were unable to drag their boat across the sand dunes to the water. By this time, Sturt and his team were sick and starving, but still managed to row their way back up the Murray River.

Sturt undertook these journeys in the summer, when the heat and dryness of western New South Wales is at its peak. His report of finding land suitable for farming was one of the factors that encouraged the British government to establish the colony of South Australia.

In 1846, following his return from expeditions north of Adelaide, Sturt was able to confirm that the rivers of New South Wales did not flow into an inland sea, finally answering the question that had intrigued explorers for decades. This was the first exploration of Australia's great deserts by a European, and Sturt and his team became very ill from the heat and exhaustion. They found Sturt's Stony Desert and established that Cooper Creek did not flow into an inland sea, but simply dwindled and stopped flowing in the desert.

Top: Sturt's Stony Desert
Above: Sturt's Stony Desert today

Crossing the Deserts

What Inspired the Explorers of Australia's Deserts?

- They wanted to find overland routes that linked the colonies with each other. Since there were no roads linking New South Wales, South Australia and Western Australia, people living in these colonies could only contact each other by letters sent on ships.
- They wanted to discover more land for farming beyond the deserts.
- They needed to find routes to lay the tracks for railways, and cables for telegraph lines.
- The idea that humans had to conquer nature, rather than live in harmony with it, was a driving force amongst the explorers of the 18th and 19th centuries.
- Australia's desert explorers were the celebrities of their era.

LUDWIG LEICHHARDT

Leichhardt was an explorer who was a celebrity of his time. Crowds farewelled him on his expeditions and people waited eagerly to find out what he would discover. The local paper reported that, 'His portrait adorns the window of every shop'.

In 1844, Leichhardt travelled from Jimbour in the Darling Downs in Queensland across to Port Essington on the Northern Territory coast. His reports of the lush land in the north of Queensland resulted in settlers deciding to establish farms there.

In 1848, he left Moreton Bay in Queensland, hoping to travel across the country to the Swan River Settlement in Western Australia. This expedition involved crossing massive desert areas. He disappeared on this journey and no trace of what happened to him has ever been found.

THINK ABOUT IT

What do you think happened to Ludwig Leichhardt? What would happen today if a celebrity disappeared in the Australian desert?

EDWARD JOHN EYRE

Eyre wanted to become the first European to travel overland from Sydney to Adelaide. He achieved this aim in 1838, droving a large herd of cattle and sheep all the way. This journey showed that it was possible to keep sheep and cattle alive when taking them overland to settlements in South Australia, rather than loading them onto ships to transport them there.

In 1839, Eyre became the first European to see the salt lake now called Kati Thanda-Lake Eyre. The next year he set out to explore the Great Australian Bight and the Nullarbor. Travelling from Streaky Bay in South Australia to Albany in Western Australia, he managed to survive the arid conditions, helped by Wylie, an Aboriginal member of the expedition.

Below: Salt Flats at Lake Eyre

Australia South to North

The deserts of inland Australia were an enormous barrier to further expansion of settlement in the 1800s. The Victorian government offered a prize of £2000 to the first explorer to travel from the south to the north of the continent. Three great explorers, Stuart, Burke and Wills took on the challenge of attempting to reach the northern coast by an overland route from the south. Their achievements resulted in the expansion of settlement into the Northern Territory.

JOHN MCDOUALL STUART

John McDouall Stuart is remembered in Australia's exploration history for being the first explorer to cross the continent from south to north, confirming that it was possible to reach the northern coast by land. The harsh desert terrain, lack of water and extreme heat made his achievement remarkable. With no telephones or any way of contacting help, Stuart's team was completely on its own during the journey. His previous attempts to reach the north of Australia had failed, but Stuart's third attempt was more successful. He left from Adelaide in October 1861, and reached the Indian Ocean on the northern coast near the site of Darwin in July 1862. Sick and blinded in one eye, Stuart then turned around and travelled back to Adelaide.

The Result of Stuart's Discoveries

Although he had to cross inhospitable deserts, Stuart also found areas that were suitable for pasturing livestock. The result of this discovery was that settlers began moving into the Northern Territory, and the town of Palmerston, later renamed Darwin, was established in 1869. The Overland Telegraph Line followed the route of Stuart's journey, and enabled Australia to be linked to Britain. He received the £2000 award that had been offered by the Victorian Government for being the first to reach the north.

Top: John McDouall Stuart
Above: Kings Canyon Northern Territory

BURKE & WILLS

In August 1860, Robert Burke and William Wills left Melbourne on an expedition to the Gulf of Carpentaria. At Cooper Creek in Queensland they left some of the team behind and continued on northwards. Those left behind were instructed to wait three months until they returned. The journey was very difficult but Burke and Wills did reach the Gulf in December. On the return journey, they arrived at their Cooper Creek camp only hours after the others had left, thinking that Burke and Wills might have perished.

Leaving a note behind at the abandoned camp, Burke and Wills attempted to travel to the small settlement at Mount Hopeless, where they thought they would find help. They both died on this last journey.

Clockwise: Crossing Lodden Plains, Camp at Coopers Creek, Crossing the Stony Desert, Arrival at Carpentaria, 1860

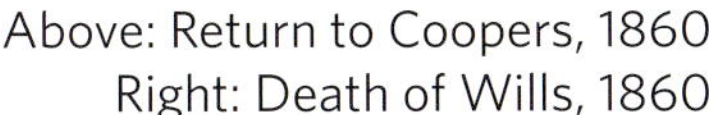

Above: Return to Coopers, 1860
Right: Death of Wills, 1860

The Result of the Exploration to the North by Burke and Wills

Burke and Wills had not reached as far north as Stuart's expedition did a year later. Since they both died on the way, they were not able to report back on their findings. Most of what is known about their journey comes from the diary kept by Wills.

BURKE&WILLS
150 YEARS CROSSING AUSTRALIA 2010
AUSTRALIA 60c

Exploring Australia's West

The enormous distances, extensive deserts and harsh climate kept the western interior of Australia a mystery to Europeans until the 1870s. When a few adventurous explorers finally managed to cross the deserts, what they found beyond them was perfect cattle country. Australia's export cattle industry still operates from these areas.

ERNEST GILES

Ernest Giles made his first attempt to cross from South Australia to the western coast in 1873. Leaving from near Oodnadatta, he had to turn back when faced with the Gibson Desert. In 1875, he tried again, this time crossing the Nullarbor and reaching Perth six months later. This was not enough for Giles and, after resting for two months, he crossed from Geraldton on the western coast back to South Australia. This time he did not let the Gibson Desert stop him.

Above: Ernest Giles, 1873

THE FORREST BROTHERS

In 1870, John Forrest left Perth to travel to Adelaide. The route he took was more inland than that travelled by John Eyre thirty years before. Because of this slight change he was able to discover the farmland that Eyre had missed. In 1874, Forrest set out again, this time tackling the daunting Gibson Desert. John Forrest entered politics in later life and became the first Premier of Western Australia in 1890.

In 1879, Alexander Forrest, John's younger brother, explored the Kimberley region and realised it was perfect for cattle grazing. His reports on the area resulted in the birth of the cattle industry in Western Australia's north. Based on his reports, cattle owners drove their cattle across from the eastern colonies and settled in the Kimberley region. Some of these journeys took years to complete and are legendary in the state's history.

Both the Forrest brothers were born near Bunbury in Western Australia.

Above left: John Forrest, 1874
Above right: Alexander Forrest, 1874

The 1873 race across the desert

WILLIAM GOSSE AND PETER WARBURTON

William Gosse was a surveyor for the South Australian government. In 1873, he was asked to find a route from Alice Springs to Perth. Although he led the official expedition, another privately funded team, led by Peter Warburton, was attempting to do exactly the same thing. In competition to be the first to reach Perth, both men tried to avoid each other along the way.

Gosse was the first European to see Uluru, naming it Ayers Rock. Gosse and the expedition's camel driver, Kamran, both climbed the rock, unaware of the disrespect they were showing to a place of great spiritual significance to the Aboriginal people. Gosse explored as far as King's Canyon in the Northern Territory and then had to turn back, beaten by the desert conditions. Warburton pushed on, crossing the Great Sandy Desert and reaching the Western Australian coast.

Above: Major Warburton, 1874
Below: Uluru today

Modern Explorers
20th and 21st Centuries

Australian Antarctic Territory

DOUGLAS MAWSON

In 1911, Douglas Mawson led Australia's first expedition to the Antarctic. Like the explorers of Australia before him, he charted the coastlines and explored the land, including Macquarie Island. In 1912, his two fellow explorers died, leaving Mawson to make his way back to Main Base alone. This journey through the ice and snow lasted thirty days. A replica of Mawson's Hut has been built in Hobart to show how he and his team lived during their Antarctic expeditions. Mawson's image is on Australia's one hundred dollar note.

The Result of Mawson's Explorations

Antarctica was the last unknown continent when Mawson went there in 1911. Driven by his interest in scientific research, Mawson's discoveries covered geology, biology and meteorology. He also claimed land there for his country, just as explorers sailing to Australia had done centuries before. Many nations wanted a part of Antarctica, and The Antarctic Treaty was signed by twelve countries in 1959, including Australia.

Above left: Sir Douglas Mawson, 1911
Below: Antarctica today

Space exploration

There are three NASA astronauts who were born in Australia. They are Andy Thomas, Paul Scully-Power and Phil Chapman.

Scientists working at Australia's telescopes at Parkes and Siding Springs are involved in space research. Although they will never go to the stars, they can still explore them using technology. The Canberra Deep Space Communication Complex at Tidbinbilla is one of NASA's three Deep Space Networks in the world. They provide communications between NASA missions and teams on Earth.

Clockwise: Andy Thomas, Phil Chapman, Paul Scully-Power

ACTIVITIES FOR FUTURE SPACE EXPLORERS

How are space explorers different from the explorers in Australia's history? Points to think about:

- Communication methods
- Distances to travel
- Sources of food and water
- Vehicles
- Clothing

How are space explorers the same as the explorers in Australia's history? Points to think about:

- Claiming territory
- Looking for resources to exploit
- The human quest for more knowledge
- Expansion of human settlement

Australia's Exploration Timeline

60,000 YEARS AGO

Ancestors of the Australian Aboriginal people arrive

1606

Luis de Torres finds the Torres Strait

1606

Willem Jansz finds the northern coast

1616

Dirk Hartog leaves a pewter plate on an island off Western Australia

1642

Abel Tasman finds Tasmania

1770

James Cook finds the eastern coast and claims it for Britain

1788

Governor Phillip explores around Sydney

1801-1803

Matthew Flinders circumnavigates Australia

1817-1818

John Oxley explores inland New South Wales

1824

Hume and Hovell explore south to Port Phillip (Melbourne)

1846

Charles Sturt confirms there is no inland sea

1848

Ludwig Leichhardt disappears trying to reach the Swan River Settlement (Perth) from Queensland

1861

Burke and Wills die in the desert

1862

John McDouall Stuart becomes the first explorer to reach the northern coast overland from Adelaide

1911

Douglas Mawson explores Antarctica and claims land for Australia

Glossary

WORD	MEANING
circumnavigate	sail all the way around something
droving cattle	travelling overland with cattle
dwindle	slowly decrease
geologist	person who studies rocks
inadequate	not good enough
inhospitable	unwelcoming
irrigation	water or agriculture
lieutenant	rank in the armed forces
meteorology	science of the weather
squatters	settlers who claimed land
terrain	area of land with particular features

Index